Reflecting

Embracing the Creator's Design

Valorie Bender Quesenberry

Indianapolis, Indiana

Published by Wesleyan Publishing House
Indianapolis, Indiana 46250
Printed in the United States of America
ISBN: 978-0-89827-428-8

To the Reader

I write to you as a friend—as a fellow journeyer on the trek toward knowing God in new and intimate ways. Like you, I have a longing to know who He is, what He wants from me, what He has planned for me. So I've been getting to know the many women whose stories appear in His Word, and I have come to understand many new truths about the real purpose God had when He created woman.

I invite you on this journey of discovery. We'll meet women from varied circumstances who found God faithful and true to His word, sisters in faith who faced the same struggles we face.

This is a journey that has a great deal of relevance to our lives today. So you'll also read brief snippets from women of our time who are demonstrating what it means to put Bible lessons into practice.

You may choose to take this journey alone or as part of a small group or Bible class. If you take it alone, I challenge you to find a trusted friend who can help you process the decisions you'll make along the way. If you choose to take this journey as part of a group meeting, take time before your meeting to read "For Openers," "Getting to Know Her," and the Scripture passage for that week.

So, come on. Let me introduce you to some amazing sisters, women who touched the heart of God.

To the Leader

I hope you're excited about this journey. The women of the Bible have so much to teach women today. As leader, you'll have the privilege of shepherding group members in their discussions and in their commitments. It is important that you prepare personally for each session by reading the text and by praying for God's guidance and leadership.

The first two sections of each week's session—**For Openers** and **Getting to Know Her**—should take about one-fourth of your total session time. Reading and discussing the next two sections—**The Word Speaks** and **Where We Come In**—along with the sidebars will make up the majority of your session. Try to leave about a quarter of your session time on the response sections—**Responding through Prayer**, **My Next Step**, and **Keep It in Mind**.

After the first week, begin each session by asking participants how they applied the previous week's commitments. Encourage the group to share freely about their successes and struggles and to support one another. Do this shepherding prayerfully and with the grace and compassion that can flow only from a relationship with Jesus Christ.

May God's presence be felt in your group and its members come to know Him in new and fresh ways.

Contents

Acknowledgements

I am indebted to those who have helped me discover and clarify the concepts in this book. I am especially grateful for:

The eloquent discussion of beauty in the book, *Captivating,* by John and Stasi Eldredge, which shaped my thinking on this fascinating topic.

My sisters in faith who inspire me with your friendship and reflect Him in your beauty. How special you are.

My father, James Bender, Jr., whose cherishing love nurtures me still, and my mother, Sherry Bender, whose pattern of godly womanhood guides me daily.

My brother, Jim, whose keen perception aided my study.

My brother, Danny, whose sensitivity reflects the Father.

My "sister," Joy, who shares my heritage and quest for truth.

Stephanie, whose counseling insight was so helpful.

Susan, who assisted me with many details.

Jerry, whose mentoring and encouragement bless me.

Kevin, whose editorial work is skillful and thoughtful.

Ashley, Autumn, Stewart, and Kaley, who give me joy.

Duane, whose strength and love are God's gifts to me. I love your warrior heart.

My Heavenly Father, whose daughter I delight in being. These truths are Yours.

Introduction

Writing a book on beauty is akin to running the gauntlet. If the author is beautiful, the readers will want to know her secret but may feel she cannot identify with their struggles. If she is unattractive, the readers may assume she is trying to assuage her wounded pride.

Like you, I'm quite average, I suppose. I've known my share of struggles, and I have no great beauty secrets to share. Instead, I want to study with you some amazing truths in the Word of God which address the issues of beauty and femininity and how they impact our relationships.

We will see the Father's heart for His daughters and understand why He created us with the desire to be beautiful. We will examine how beauty affects our relationships with friends and family as well as our relationship with our Heavenly Father.

Why Beauty?

It seems a trivial theme for a book unless you understand how significant beauty is to the feminine perspective. The desire to be beautiful is the expression of a woman's instinctive understanding that she was created to reflect the majesty of God.

Elisabeth Elliot says, "the soul is feminine." John and Stasi Eldredge write about "a soulish beauty." The recognition that beauty is the core of femininity is vital to understanding the nature of a woman.

Women's appearance is always a current topic. That's because God made beauty to be a visible stamp of His image on His daughters, and it attracts us. Sin and self-centeredness often lead to improper use of beauty, but beauty itself was created as a good thing.

What Is Beauty?

It is said that beauty is in the eye of the beholder. Yet, there are some generally accepted standards of beauty in any culture. In our western society, this has to do with symmetry of features, health, and fitness. Beyond that, beauty may also be defined as the result of a woman's efforts to make herself attractive. In this study, we will use these definitions interchangeably. Though there are few who are blessed with true outward beauty, most of us at least try to look pretty. And in that way, we lay a small claim to beauty.

Wanting Beauty

"You have to suffer to be beautiful." My mother used to repeat these wise words to me as I resisted her efforts to wind my not-naturally-curly hair on rollers. And, like all women, I have discovered she spoke the truth—thanks to the imperfections of the genetic code and the effects of aging, beauty requires a little tender loving care.

Why do we "suffer?" Why do women sacrifice money, time, and personal comfort for beauty? Is it innate feminine vanity? Is it the corruption of sin? Is it one of the ways the female discovered to secure male protection and a father for her children?

No, the desire for beauty is so basic to the nature of women that females in every century and every culture have pursued it. It is a component of feminine design.

A misunderstanding of this important concept has confused and sabotaged Christian women in our efforts to follow Christ while at the same time recognizing our inner desire for affirmation. The corruption of beauty in our culture has caused us to mistake our desire as sinful. The ambivalence of the church in its approach to women's issues of beauty has complicated the matter. Yet, the Bible does address the subject of women's beauty—both in principle and example.

As we study the awesome words of our God, I hope you will more fully understand God's heart of love for His daughters—the wonderful, fascinating, exquisite creation He fashioned from an ordinary rib, a human impression of the grandeur of His nature, the feminine counterpart to man. I trust you will be empowered to resist the destructive messages of the culture which exploit beauty as a means of power and measure of worth. I invite you to celebrate the beauty God has imprinted into your very being and let it reflect in your appearance and in your relationships. The Father has monogrammed His beauty on you. He delights in you.

"The LORD your God is with you, he is mighty to save. He will take great delight in you, he will quiet you with his love, he will rejoice over you with singing" (Zeph. 3:17).

1

The Halo Effect

Isaiah 62:1–5

From Zion, perfect in beauty, God shines forth.
—Psalm 50:2

Discovery

Beauty has power—it is God's artistry displayed in His daughters.

For Openers

"Once upon a time, there was a beautiful princess who lived in a lovely palace . . ." There is nothing like a princess story to intrigue little girls (and grown girls, too). Gauzy gowns, glittery tiaras, stardust, and magical evenings—it's more than playing dress-up; it's a fascination that adult women still carry somewhere in a wistful little place they rarely talk about.

Why a princess? It is unusual to find a little girl who wants to be the queen. No, the princess is the one she dreams of being. You see, a princess has a father, the king, who cherishes, protects, and delights in her. And every woman instinctively knows that's what she was made for—princess living. It is rooted in the feminine soul.

In the fairy tales, the princess is always beautiful. She is not corrupted by her beauty; it is a vital part of her essence. But more than that, she is kind, sweet, and gentle. In real life, beauty isn't always matched by a lovely temperament. But people do tend to think that other traits of an attractive person are just as attractive and desirable.

There is a psychological term for this bias—it's called *the Halo effect.*

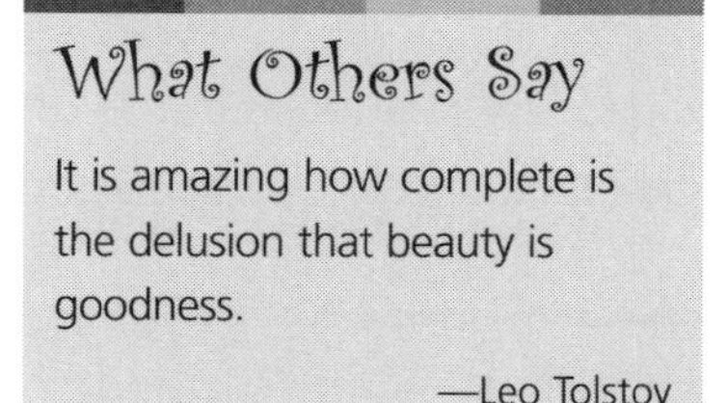
What Others Say

It is amazing how complete is the delusion that beauty is goodness.

—Leo Tolstoy

What gives physical beauty such power? Or rather who did? The answer, of course, is God—the Creator of all things. Let's take a look at the woman who first mirrored the beauty of her Maker.

Getting to Know Her

She was conceived in the heart of God and fashioned with His own hands. It's interesting that God put Adam to sleep while He created her. Maybe this was to give him a delightful surprise; maybe it was to bestow on her a certain mystique, the aura of femininity that is God's own signature in the soul of every woman.

Whatever the reason, when Adam woke up, he was properly appreciative. Long before the great poets penned their sonnets, Adam spoke beautiful words of bonding over his new bride. He called her *Isha*—woman, taken from man.

The creation of woman showcased God's loving design. God is all about relationship. He intended the beauty of woman to be part of this plan. He created man and woman to enjoy relationship with Him and with each other. The characteristics he gave to each sex were to mirror His complex being and to enable them to complement each other in the marriage relationship. God expressed His strength in the creation of man; He displayed His beauty in the design of woman. Together, these attributes tell us something about the God who is the very essence of all that is good. "Honor and majesty surround him; strength and beauty fill his sanctuary" (Ps. 96:6 NLT).

Same-sex relationships are offensive to God, because they do not give a balanced representation of His being. "So God created man

How It Works Today

Nikki was a tomboy. She preferred playing ball with the boys to wearing the frilly dresses and dainty shoes her mother bought for her. As she matured, she struggled with her identity as a woman. The culture was stressing free love and the unisex ideology and this added to her confusion. Entering college to earn her Bachelor of Science in Nursing degree, Nikki was swept up into feminist thinking. Resenting the condescension of doctors, nurses were uniting under the banner of disdain for men. Though Nikki was from a solid Christian home, she found herself adopting the thought patterns of those in her classes.

Nikki graduated and married Lyle, a godly man, strong in his own identity and possessing a deep love for his new wife. When they clashed and she resisted her role, he simply loved her enough to be calm and unchanged, gently showing her the warrior love Christ has for His bride.

Nikki found that his strength enabled her to embrace her own femininity. Today, married over twenty-five years with children and grandchildren, Nikki and Lyle have a beautiful relationship that portrays the strength and beauty principle. Nikki treasures the comment Lyle once made, "Nikki is the heart of our home."

in his own image, in the image of God he created him; male and female he created them" (Gen. 1:27). It takes both genders—male and female—in a covenant relationship to accurately portray His majestic image.

God intends the majesty of His being and the beauty in the world He created to draw us into relationship with Him. "For since the creation of the world God's invisible qualities—his eternal power and divine nature—have been clearly seen, being understood from what has been made, so that men are without excuse" (Rom. 1:20). He wants the beauty of His nature to pull us toward Him.

Just as the beauty of God draws us into a relationship with Him, the beauty of woman was intended to draw the man to her. God gave Eve breathtaking beauty and put into Adam a desire to partake of that beauty through a relationship. More than mere sexual fulfillment, the beauty of a woman fills up a man emotionally and makes him feel complete in his soul.

Enter Satan—cast from heaven, stripped of his glory. He understands that God designed women to be the bearers of beauty in His world. He does not love their beauty; he desires to seize it and ruin its power. He hates anything that reflects the glory of God and especially loathes relationships, since they are the loving essence of God's character. That makes beauty, in all its forms, his special target. In their book, *Captivating*, John and Stasi Eldredge suggest that his hatred comes from jealousy:

> **What Others Say**
>
> In every man's heart there is a secret nerve that answers to the vibrations of beauty.
>
> —Christopher Morley

> Satan fell because of his beauty. Now his heart for revenge is to assault beauty. He destroys it in the natural world whenever he can. Strip mines, oil spills, fires, Chernobyl. He wreaks destruction on the glory of God in the earth like a psychopath committed to destroying great works of art. But, most especially, he hates Eve. Because she is captivating, uniquely glorious, and he cannot be. She is the incarnation of the Beauty of God. More than anything else in all creation, she embodies the glory of God. She allures the world to God. He hates it with a jealousy we can only imagine.[1]

As women who now live in a world that is Satan's dominion, we feel the attacks on our femininity and the tilt of the culture toward exploitation of beauty. Understanding why we were made to be beautiful is so important to our relationships and our emotional and spiritual health.

Bible Background

"Like a gold ring in a pig's snout is a beautiful woman who shows no discretion" (Prov. 11:22).

It is taken for granted here that beauty or comeliness of body is as a jewel of gold, a thing very valuable, and, where there is wisdom and grace to guard against the temptations of it, it is a great ornament.

—Matthew Henry

Women have this deep intuitiveness that we were made to reflect the beauty of the Creator and to respond to it in our world. Those who would dismiss the female awareness of beauty as frivolous and shallow are at best, uneducated, and at worst, ignorant of God's design of women. Beauty of face and form, beauty of the soul and spirit—it is the core of femininity. It is what we were made for.

The Word Speaks

When God wanted a word picture to represent the value He places on His people, He chose a woman as the image. God identifies *himself* as the heroic warrior, desiring to captivate the heart of His beloved. Like a young man demonstrating his manliness, the Scripture refers to God's strong arm (Luke 1:51) and the depth of His love. *Women* have been given the honor of representing the earthly side of the Father's prized relationship with those who trust in Him. The feminine gender portrays the beauty and trusting surrender of God's people. Strength and beauty are bonded. In the Old Testament, this covenant was exclusively with the Jewish nation; after Jesus' death, anyone who trusted Christ was included.

As the choice jewel representing Israel, the Bible refers to the capital city of Jerusalem as the daughter of Zion—the princess of Palestine. There are multiple Old Testament references that use this feminine imagery. Jeremiah 6:2 says, "I have likened the daughter of Zion to a comely and delicate woman" (KJV).

God could have used another form of symbolism, but He chose to depict a woman, made in the beauty of His image, gifted with a feminine perspective, a treasure to be protected and cherished.

Read **Isaiah 62:1-5**. Notice the symbolism in these verses and how God compares His joy to the emotions of a wedding day. How does the metaphor make this passage come alive for you?

Some feminists protest chivalry—male consideration for and protection of women. Study Isaiah 51:16. God says that He has kept Zion safe in His hand, like a groom tenderly watching over his bride. What does this analogy teach us about the protecting role of a man in a woman's life?

In Mark 2:19, Jesus refers to himself as "the bridegroom." Have someone read Ephesians 5:31–32 and Revelation 19:7–9. To whom does "the bride" refer in these passages?

Turn to Revelation 21:2. How does John's metaphor for the holy city compare with the Old Testament description of Jerusalem, the daughter of Zion? Isn't it interesting that God understands the "making an entrance" thing? Women everywhere identify with the doors swinging open as they present themselves lavishly prepared for their bridegroom. Though this is speaking about the Church's holy beauty as she is presented to Christ, it tells us that God understands the female psyche. He made us, and He uses this imagery to describe the Church's joy at being presented to Christ when He returns.

Where We Come In

The beauty of the natural world draws us into a relationship with God. The beauty of a woman has power which influences each of her relationships. God created beauty to be a force for good, to reflect His majestic nature.

Scripture validates the power of beauty. Many women in the Scripture are described as beautiful—Sarah, Rebekah, Rachel, Abigail, Bathsheba, Tamar, Vashti, Esther, and Job's daughters are among those. In each case, the Bible records that they were fair to look upon, not judging their beauty as either positive or negative. Their stories tell what effect their beauty had. Like gravity, the power of beauty simply is—the effect of its power is determined by the conduct of the owner.

Human experience teaches us that beauty has intrinsic power. It is the force behind great art and classic music. It attracts us to certain people and may even convince us to buy products they endorse. It makes a favorable first impression even if we don't know anything about the person behind the face. It causes us to desire a relationship with someone so naturally gifted.

What Others Say

Personal beauty is a greater recommendation than any letter of reference.

—Aristotle

[Beauty is] a sort of bloom on a woman. If you have it you don't need to have anything else; and if you don't have it, it doesn't much matter what else you have.

—James Matthew Barrie

Beauty also has destructive power. It has been the cause of feuds, duels, and epic battles. It has destroyed families, separated friends, and lured men into heartache.

And the visceral reaction to beauty begins early—basically from birth. Even young children notice beauty in nature and in people.

The research quoted here seems to confirm that recognition and appreciation of beauty is hardwired into the human brain, proving that even from infancy, beauty has power.

Did You Know?

Researchers in the UK have confirmed that babies as young as two-days old prefer to gaze at attractive faces. When the babies were shown paired images of female faces, they spent a longer amount of time fixed on the more attractive face. "'Attractiveness is not simply in the eye of the beholder, it is in the brain of the newborn infant right from the moment of birth and possibly prior to birth,' the University of Exeter researcher said."

—BBC Online

God's Word gives examples of both positive and negative effects of beauty.

Read the story of Sarah (Sarai) in Genesis 12:11–20. Think about how the power of beauty caused Abram to fear for his life.

Look at 1 Samuel 25:3–35. In verse 3, what adjective beside *beautiful* is used to describe Abigail? How does her story validate that she used the power of her beauty in a wise way?

Read 1 Corinthians 6:20. Think about how this verse applies to personal beauty.

As women, we reach out for beauty, desiring its affirmation on our self-worth, wanting the positive power it holds over our relationships with others. But when we place the focus on acquiring beauty as an end in itself, we end up discontented and disillusioned. Beauty was never meant to be a personal obsession, but rather a reflection of our Father who asks us to surrender its power to His lavish love.

Responding through Prayer

In a moment of silence, imagine you are looking at yourself in a mirror. Instead of just assessing your flaws, search for the beauty God created in you. Speak words of surrender as you mentally place the mirror in His hands. Watch for His reaction; listen to His words. You are beautiful; you are unique; you are loved. The Creator admires you, His beautiful piece of art.

My Next Step

This week, I will be watchful for Satan's assault. He will tempt me either to self-loathing or personal pride. When I am under attack, I will:

-
-

Keep It in Mind

A halo is *an atmosphere or quality of glory, majesty, and sanctity*. That's how God has crowned His daughters, each of them. He has placed in each female body the best of His artistry and in each feminine soul the desire for relationship. This is the beauty of His image reflected in you.

"Your hands made me and formed me; give me understanding to learn your commands" (Ps. 119:73).

2

Daddy's Eyes, Father's Heart

Ezekiel 16:1–32, 59–63

The splendor I had given you made your beauty perfect, declares the Sovereign LORD.

—Ezekiel 16:14

Discovery

God delights in the beauty of His daughters and wants them to accept His cherishing love.

For Openers

There are a few photos of my teen years that make me shudder. You probably have a few too. The trial and error attempts at beauty are painful to view. At this tender age, it wasn't enough that our families thought we were beautiful, we craved the admiration of others, our peers, who could give us the ultimate acceptance.

In a spiritual sense, mature women still struggle with that syndrome. No matter the affirmation of the Father, we yearn for the admiration of earthly eyes. Sometimes, we cannot keep our balance. It may leave us depressed and dispassionate about life, or it could cause us to self-destruct. That's how it was with Sunny.

Getting to Know Her

Sunny was a prodigal, a beauty refugee. But it hadn't always been that way, not when she was at her father's house. Even when she was wearing muddy barn clothes, Sunny knew she was beautiful to her father. She'd been secure in his house and in his heart. But it hadn't been enough for her; she wanted to hear the words and see the admiration that others could give.

She cringed as she remembered her demanding words, her careless attitude. She'd taken the money he'd saved for her and hopped on the first bus bound for the city.

The glitter and gold she imagined was replaced with glaring reality when her cash starting running out. Luckily, she had a friend in photography who promised her big bucks. But though she bared her beauty to the hunger of a million lenses, not once had the flash of the camera made her feel lovely. She couldn't take the guilt; she turned to drugs to keep her from remembering love and home.

Then came the day she collapsed, strung out; they found a fresh face to replace her. Alone and destitute, there was only one way a wasted woman could find work, if that's what you called this nightmare of leering eyes and stinking rooms. It made her feel dirtier than the pigpen at home. Sunny sat on the rumpled covers and remembered the farm where even the staff was treated with dignity. Her wounded pride didn't matter much now; she was so over the empty glamour.

So, she went home. Dirty, sick, and oh, so tired. It was springtime in the country and tiny shoots of green poked through the ground to greet her. She wasn't sure if she wanted her daddy to see her or not. Maybe she could just duck into the staff entrance. But he didn't let her.

While she shuffled up the driveway, he exploded from the house, running to hug her as only daddies can hug their little girls. And when she finally lifted shame-filled eyes to his face, she saw the most amazing truth. His love and forgiveness made her beautiful again.

Jesus gave us the parable of the prodigal son. The truth it speaks is similar to an allegory in Ezekiel 16, where God compares the nation of Israel to a woman's rebellion and restoration.

God uses the imagery of a baby girl, abandoned at birth and discovered by one who raised her with lavish care.

Did You Know?

In ancient times, female babies were often considered undesirable and left exposed in the elements or thrown out on the rubbish heap to die. Satan has always nurtured the culture's abuse of God's daughters. Name some of the twenty-first century "rubbish heaps."

The girl grew to womanhood, known everywhere for her beauty. One day, she stopped valuing the love that had given her life and instead depended on her own features to bring her self-worth. She "trusted in her beauty" and began to market herself, using her luxurious gifts to make her more appealing to a demanding audience.

What Others Say

In His inexorable love He demonstrated exactly what He had had in mind by calling himself a Bridegroom—the Initiator, Protector, Provider, Lover—and Israel His bride, His beloved. He rescued her, called her by name, wooed and won her, grieved when she went whoring after other gods.

—Elisabeth Elliot

But though she used everything she knew to gain admiration, it was in vain. No one wanted her favors (v. 34). Putting all her focus on others' opinion of her beauty was foolish and destructive. But when she returned to the one who loved her unconditionally she found restoration and affirmation.

The Word Speaks

Read **Ezekiel 16:1-32** and **59-63**.

How might the description of the abandoned baby in verses 3–5 be applied to us before we came to Christ? We were cast aside by Satan, the refuse of his rage at God and His perfect creation. Rather than loving us, Satan despises us (v. 5). Should this fact make us view our twisted culture's beauty "rules" in a different light?

Who came to rescue the little girl? Who loved her for her true worth?

In verse 8, God offers the security of His protective love. When a man spread the skirt of his robe over a woman, it was a figurative expression of his covenant to protect and care for her through marriage. It was also symbolic of God's care for His own. See Ruth 2:12 and Psalm 36:7.

In Ezekiel 16:9–14, God describes how He lavishly cared for His beloved. We should notice here that the bathing and clothing and adorning were not to *make* her beautiful, but to *reveal* the value He placed on her, to demonstrate His love and delight in her. Her value *to Him* was the same when she was abandoned and destitute as when she was luxuriously dressed. But her actions later in this chapter show that she didn't get it; she didn't understand that her own intrinsic worth, not the ornaments, made her beautiful. Think about how easy it is for us to forget that our beauty is not manufactured, but innate.

Bible Background

"I spread My skirt over you and covered your nakedness" (NASB) ("spread my wing over you," NKJV), reflects the ancient custom of espousal as depicted in the book of Ruth. . . .The Hebrew word (*kanaph*) for *skirt*, means "extremity" and is used to describe the skirt or flap of a garment. In addition this word can be translated "wings" (as of a bird) and is a beautiful figurative picture in Scripture of God's "wings" protecting His own.

—Bruce Hurt

Beginning in verse 15, God describes how the woman used all He had done for her to attract the attention of other admirers. But when she left the giver's care, she discovered a strange thing. Though she begged for affirmation and love, even bribed other men for it, they didn't give it to her. They used her, but didn't want her. Though in this passage God is describing the unfaithfulness of the nation Israel in turning to other gods, there is an applicable lesson. What happens when women turn from the affirmation of the Creator and seek admiration from the shallow culture?

Read Exodus 34:14. God describes himself as jealous of our devotion. Because He is holy and perfect, the jealousy God has is not self-centered.

> **What Others Say**
>
> Envy is wanting something that belongs to another person . . . jealousy is wanting what is rightfully yours.
>
> —Tommy Nelson

Is He jealous when His daughters seek admiration from a culture engineered by Satan? What do you think is the motivation for this divine emotion?

Where We Come In

Just like the biblical story, little girls in our world are often abandoned, neglected, and abused. These early experiences affect our internal sense of self-worth. Can you identify circumstances in your past which have affected your sense of personal value?

The Scripture uses an extreme example of prostitution to describe Israel's pursuit of admiration. While this might not apply to us, in what ways have women today sought to find affirmation through culture's definition of physical beauty?

What price do the beauty "rules" of our culture demand from us?

Read Psalm 45:8–17. Describe what these verses say about God's heart for His daughter, Israel. How might the sentiments of these verses apply to us today?

Satan wants to consume beauty; God desires to nourish beauty. Satan says barter your beauty; God says consecrate your beauty. Satan says you're not good enough; God says you're made in His image.

Real beauty awareness begins with the Father. He has cared for you since you first opened your eyes in your mother's womb. He delighted with the first pink ribbon tied around that wispy little-girl ponytail. He watched you admire your first pair of white patent leather shoes. He loved you with your too-big-for-your-face front teeth and gangly adolescent body. He saw you struggle with acne and braces and weight issues. He knew about the breathlessness you felt when the dreamy guy gave you an admiring glance. He's been there through bad hair styles and weird fashions and premature aging. He sees the woman you've become and knows the power of the unique beauty He has given you—that's the Father who waits by the sofa for you to open the front door. He'll wrap you in His embrace and tell you the truth—He really does think you're beautiful.

Having a restored relationship with Him is the first step in coming to a place of contentment with who you are. Being secure in Him gives you the right perspective to discover the incredible value you have and to celebrate the power of your beauty.

How It Works Today

Elaine is a woman with a mission: to encourage women to understand their value in Christ. God has given her a two-pronged ministry—as a counselor to women targeted by the abortion industry and as an organizer of women's support groups throughout the county.

Elaine has worked for almost twenty years as a volunteer counselor at a center that supports women with pregnancy crises. She has listened to young girls spill their stories of sexual abuse; she has watched them battle the false affirmation of promiscuous sex; she has seen the emotional and spiritual devastation suffered by post-abortive clients; she has witnessed how the search for admiration has flung women into STD's, harmful relationships, and heart-wrenching decisions about unborn babies. She cries with them, prays with them, loves them—she wages her own war with the culture Satan delights in.

Elaine also motivates women to realize their worth by being part of a women's movement that encourages sisterhood and spiritual development. As a spokesperson for Christian women, she speaks to women's gatherings and mentors other women in leadership as well as being the force behind an annual Christian women's retreat. Elaine knows the truth—real worth as a woman comes from knowing the Father and opening our souls to His gentle embrace.

Responding through Prayer

Listen for His voice as you pray silently. *Father, You made me to reflect Your beauty. Thank You for being there through my personal journey. Show me how I have turned from Your gaze and sought affirmation inappropriately from the culture. Please give me an awareness of Your faithful, cherishing love for me. When I feel unlovely and unworthy, remind me to look into Your eyes.*

My Next Step

This week I will remember that the Father loves me first and best. I am cherished in His house. When I am tempted to lean out the window to catch substitute admiration, I will:

-

-

Keep It in Mind

Part of the reason we reach for substitute affirmation is that we can see human eyes, but we can't see the Father's. He asks us to be like Sarah, a beautiful woman whose name is chiseled in the halls of faith. She had the temerity to believe God would affirm her womanhood through a pregnancy when it was physiologically impossible. Though she botched it a few times, she didn't turn from the Father's affirmation. "You are her daughters if you do what is right and do not give way to fear" (1 Pet. 3:6).

3

Filter the Beauty Spam

Proverbs 31:10–31

Charm is deceptive, and beauty is fleeting.

—Proverbs 31:30

Discovery

We can use God's Word to filter the culture's false beauty messages.

For Openers

Spam is digital trash. Unlike our computer inboxes, our minds don't have a "spam" tab for discarding unwanted messages. Because this is Satan's kingdom, he will flood our minds with the destructive words he wants us to believe.

The culture daily spews these false messages:

1. Outward beauty is a mirror of the soul.

2. Outward beauty is a measure of worth.

3. Outward beauty is a means of power.

But God gave us a powerful tool in His Word; the Bible is the most effective "filter" for any false message. It is absolute truth. Basing our philosophies and self concept in His Word daily is a practice that will help us recognize the beauty malware Satan creates to attack us.

Getting to Know Her

Beauty spam is not a new thing. In ancient Palestine, this message was making the rounds. The wise man, Solomon, had a lot to say about women who modeled this kind of false message. They didn't have Hollywood or Internet pornography, but they did have harlots or prostitutes—women trapped by Satan's lies about beauty.

Prostitutes present the image that all they are is a luring face and willing body. Their focus is the attraction of the outside. Their way of making money bypasses the fact that women are so much more than a decorative exterior. And in this way, they represent the antithesis of the Bible's message about authentic beauty.

The Word Speaks

Let's look at some of the false beauty messages found in ancient times that we still encounter on a daily basis. Then we'll discover together a true beauty message found in the Bible.

FALSE: Outward beauty is a mirror of the soul.

Look at **Proverbs 6:20-28**. The woman presented here is the embodiment of this lie. Her outward appearance is the focus of her activities; she presents an image that says, "if you get my body, you get me. My appearance is the core of who I am, the soul of me."

Prostitution is the embodiment of the false beauty message that says a woman is summed up by her physical body. But women who would never stand on a street corner have subconsciously adopted the same philosophy. Satan wants us to believe that outward beauty and the pleasure it brings is the most valuable thing about a woman. By unleashing this lie on the human family, Satan has used the power of beauty to feed the voracious appetite of self-centeredness. By tricking some into believing that women are nothing more than sexual art, he has struck a fatal blow to relationships and inflicted pain to the loving heart of God. Whenever a man succumbs to pornography or prostitution, he is underscoring the belief that outer beauty matters more than inward beauty. He is agreeing with Satan against God, and Satan loves to have comrades who join him in his anti-God philosophy.

What Others Say

By plucking her petals, you do not gather the beauty of the flower.

—Rabindranath Tagore

Read the quote above. How do these words illustrate this false beauty message?

Women have been sucker-punched by Satan. The extreme ideals of today's culture steal from women the very life blood of their beauty—it devours the soul, for every woman knows that beauty is more than "skin deep." It is woven into the fabric of feminine identity.

What Others Say

Men look *at* themselves in mirrors. Women look *for* themselves.

—Elissa Melamed

The Creator knows that women's beauty will never be treasured while it remains the bartering tool of a culture. He gazes down with loving eyes and hates that many women see their beauty as a commodity and many men view it as entertainment. His heart longs for them to know the truth.

FALSE: Outward beauty is a measure of worth.

Examine **Psalm 45:3–5**; **1 Peter 1:8–19**; and **Colossians 2:13–15**.

The tales that have come down to us over time are immortal. The great romances of all time were built on the theme of the hero who saves the lady fair—from Shakespeare to Disney. We thrill to the depth of their love and shiver at the risk of the battle. We grasp just how much she is worth—how important she is—from the difficulties he endures to rescue her. He will challenge dragons, walls, armies, rivers, cliffs, and a thousand other obstacles to save the one he loves. His love is the measure of her worth.

Women are told everyday that their worth lies in the placement of their facial features or their bone structure. But, it's just another of Satan's lies. If he can keep the focus on our inadequacies, we will forget about the one who has triumphed in the greatest battle of all to win our hearts back to Him. There was no wall high enough, no heartbreak great enough, no failure deep enough to keep Him from slaying the dragon. He triumphed over it all when He struck the death blow to Satan on a cross outside Jerusalem.

My worth isn't measured by how I look but by how much I'm loved. And Jesus answered that once for all.

FALSE: Outward beauty is an acceptable means of power.

Read **Proverbs 7:21-27**. Solomon writes about men who are driven by fantasy and about women who use their charm as power. Since the beginning, women have understood that their feminine beauty and charm grants them formidable power over men. Beauty focused on domination is a manifestation of self-centeredness. The rebellious nature of sin manipulates and controls.

Read **Proverbs 31:3**. The writer is cautioning his son to be wary of getting entangled in illicit sensual pleasures. He refers to women as "those who ruin kings." What do you think prompted him to hold this opinion? What do you know about Solomon's personal life that would cause him to be cynical about women?

Now, read **Proverbs 31:10-31**. For years, I've had a thing against the Proverbs 31 woman. Christian women have been bludgeoned with her perfection ad nauseam. It probably points to our obsession with excellence, even in the spiritual realm. But it is so unlike our gracious Father to give us a checklist by which to measure our worthiness. Whether the paragon of virtue described in this chapter was a real person or just a composite image of every desirable feminine trait, it was not included in Scripture to intimidate or to depress us.

Bible Background

Solomon had suffered sorely from this quarter; and hence his repeated cautions and warnings to others. The strange woman always means one that is not a man's own; and sometimes it may also imply a foreign harlot, one who is also a stranger to the God of Israel.

—Adam Clarke

The longest portion of this passage is given to the woman's character traits and moral qualities. It is interesting that the verse dealing specifically with physical beauty is next to the last. Maybe this is to help us keep the proper perspective—God values the inward above the outward.

How does the authenticity and integrity of the woman described in this passage differ from the designing women portrayed in the media today? By making outward beauty the focus, in what ways have women relinquished their power in other areas?

Where We Come In

The false messages of beauty are progressive. First, Satan gets women to believe that they are merely a pretty package. Then he tells them that outer beauty is a measure of worth. Finally, he gets them to use their beauty for selfish means—instead of blessing others and honoring God, they trade it for gratification of power.

Christian women are not immune to false messages. We need the truth found in God's Word to diffuse the confusion about beauty's appeal.

How It Works Today

Stephanie encounters the effect of the false messages of the culture whenever she welcomes a client into her office. As a counselor, she deals with the emotional aftermath of the warped beauty ideals seen every day on glossy pages and high-def screens. Women struggling with self-worth pour out their ragged emotions; sometimes they teeter at the edge of depression.

Stephanie emphasizes the importance of accepting "today, without conditions, as is." She tells them, "improvements have no bearing on my sense of who I am and what God thinks of me today."

When we believe that we are worthless unless we become more beautiful, we validate Satan's false messages—we stamp their veracity upon our souls. Stephanie knows that women who believe improvements will make them valuable never win. It is a journey that has no ending, for there is always more improvement that could be made. So, she helps them drag the cultural lies out into the open and expose them to the affirming light of God's Word. Only when women grasp that their appearance is not a means of bartering for self-worth will they be ready to discover their true beauty.

First, we must understand the truth about beauty; then we must model it. Proverbs 31:30 says, "Charm can mislead and beauty soon fades. The woman to be admired and praised is the woman who lives in the Fear-of-GOD" (MSG). Beauty and charm are desirable; but they are temporary blessings. The loveliest and most lasting attribute of a woman is her focus on pleasing God. If she does that, her beauty will be enhanced by integrity, and her charm will be heightened by virtue.

Did You Know?

Instead of humbling herself, and putting herself into close mourning for her son, she painted her face, and tired her head, that she might appear like herself, that is (as she thought), great and majestic, hoping thereby to daunt Jehu, to put him out of countenance, and to stop his career.

—Matthew Henry

Her object was, by her royal attire, not to captivate, but to overawe Jehu.

—Jamieson-Fausset-Brown

Read **2 Kings 9:27-33**. Queen Jezebel was one of the most treacherous women in Israel's history. She manipulated her husband, King Ahab, for her own purposes. Even in her last moments of life, she tried to sway the warrior Jehu by using her feminine charm. Hearing he was coming in victory to the palace, she applied dark powder to her eyes to accentuate them and arranged her hair and leaned out the window to greet the hero, hoping to overawe him with the aura of her female beauty.

We shouldn't think that this was the only time Jezebel had used cosmetics in her beauty regimen; a woman of royalty would be well acquainted with the beauty tools of the time. I think the Bible purposefully gives this detail at this time to draw attention to her attitude, to her motive. This narrative gives us a visual on what inspired her grooming techniques at this point. How we beautify ourselves begins in the heart.

What was the motive behind Jezebel's beauty routine? What do you think she was trying to obtain—seduction, power, or both? Do you think it's ironic that here is another evil queen, just like in the fairytales?

Discuss the motive of the secular beauty culture. Is it self-centered or God-centered? Take a minute to think about the difference between using beauty to manipulate (win admiration, control men, and get favors) and regarding beauty as a way to honor God (reflect His creative design, please my husband, and delight the heart of the Father).

Feminists reject the use of feminine charm because they feel it is demeaning to a woman to resort to primal measures to get a man's attention. How do Christian women differ from them in their quest to be authentically feminine?

Responding through Prayer

Have each woman in the group anonymously write down on a slip of a paper the message she is currently battling. Put the papers in a basket and have each woman draw one out. Commit to pray for the person represented on your paper.

My Next Step

Realizing that we cannot isolate ourselves from society, we must have practical ways to filter the beauty messages of the culture. Finish the list with your own suggestions:

- Identify the false beauty messages in advertising, television, movies, and the fashion world.
- Keep a journal of what God teaches you about beauty.
-
-

Keep It in Mind

Satan has been lying to women since the garden of Eden. Defining authentic beauty with God's Word protects us "in order that Satan might not outwit us. For we are not unaware of his schemes" (2 Cor. 2:11). Satan is a hacker, but he is no match for God's security system.

4

In the Zone

Esther 2:1–17

I have chosen the way of truth; I have set my heart on your laws.

—Psalm 119:30

Discovery

Women need to know the difference between *transformation* thinking and *truth* thinking.

For Openers

Makeovers are big business. Magazines sponsor them; television shows feature them; culture embraces them. Most women are fascinated by makeovers. The fantasy world of glitter dust and admiration beckons to us. It is the *transformation zone*.

There is a reason why little girls are fascinated with Cinderella and her pumpkin-turned-coach. It is a visceral reaction to the glamour of plain turned to gorgeous. Maybe it is because we can identify with her world of cinders and difficult relationships. Maybe it is the distant memory of Eden when a beautiful woman was formed from a commonplace rib. Maybe it is the subconscious recognition that we need the dramatic power of grace in our ordinary lives.

Whatever the reason, the disillusionment we struggle with in our journey to womanhood has made us reach for the magic delight the fairy godmother brings. We adore transformation. We feel that if we can do something, rearrange something, lose something, we'll be better.

In the twenty-first century, extreme makeovers have become so common that they are considered the norm. Women are *expected* to be dissatisfied with their bodies and to continually refashion themselves in one way or another. In fact, there is almost a sense of condescension for any woman who doesn't care enough to pursue the makeover philosophy.

Today, the line between what a woman is born with and what she fashions for herself is virtually nonexistent. The public worships beauty even if it's sculpted in a surgery room or shaped by a computer techie. We enjoy the pleasure of the fantasy so much that we conveniently forget how fake it is and imagine that somewhere, somehow, just a few beauty secrets away, is the perfection that's portrayed everywhere.

What Others Say

There are no ugly women, only lazy ones.

—Helena Rubenstein

It may be difficult to distinguish between actual beauty and the artifice of it. The power of beauty is the same, whether authentic or pseudo. One corporation spelled it out plainly in their advertising slogan "Maybe she's born with it. Maybe it's Maybelline."

Even the perpetrators themselves know they are presenting a distortion. In a profession where eating disorders and surgical enhancements are the norm, models and actresses are not themselves fooled when it comes to their own appearance. Yet, the populace is subjected to cotton-candy fiction. The myth of beauty perfection haunts everyday women. And with countless images of surrogate beauties that not even the models themselves live up to, women compare themselves to an imposter; men seek the titillation of a phantom.

What Others Say

I'm not ugly, but my beauty is a total creation.

—Tyra Banks

One form of transformation gaining momentum in our culture is cosmetic surgery. From slicing off cellulite to enhancing breasts, there is a fix for anybody if you have the money. Parents give their daughters breast augmentation surgery as a high school graduation gift. Mommy makeovers are the new trend for thirty-somethings. Recently, I saw a news story on belly button makeovers. Yes, even our navels are now in jeopardy on the beauty scene. Goodbye nature; hello transformation.

What Others Say

[Media images] change our ideas about what people look like and what normal looks like . . . Our brains did not evolve with media, and many people see more media images of women than actual women. The contrast effect makes even the most beautiful non-model look less attractive; it produces a new "normal."

—Nancy Etcoff

Getting to Know Her

Read **Esther 2:1-17**.

Though Esther lived before the time of *Extreme Makeover*, she experienced a transformation in the harem of King Xerxes. This place was a modern spa and fashion set rolled into one. Angry at his queen for embarrassing him, the king of Persia conducted a huge modeling search. He sent his agents to personally round up and bring back to the palace any young girl who fit his beauty standard. There, these homegrown girls were put into Beauty 101, designed to make them fit for the king's presence.

Though we usually focus on her godly character, we have to remember that Esther was human, a normal woman. She must have enjoyed the lavish pampering. A girl who resisted such treatment would have been unlikely to win the king's heart. She was unfamiliar with the ways of the palace and humble in spirit, but we should not make her so pious that she did not feel the pull of transformation.

Did You Know?

According to the American Society of Plastic Surgery, the number one reason women have cosmetic surgery is because: They are unhappy with their body. Almost three-fourths of women surveyed said they think about their size and shape every day.

—Dr. Robert Kenevan

Perhaps the most valuable beauty tool a woman possesses is her mind. God created us to be this wonderful integration of body and spirit—one affects and enhances the other. When a woman feels beautiful, her demeanor actually enhances her appearance. If a woman believes that redesigning herself will make her more beautiful . . . it does.

Makeovers not only address the body, but also the spirit. Most women who have cosmetic surgery say they think better of themselves afterward; their self-worth benefits. But it is debatable whether this euphoria stems more from the physical changes or the woman's attitude about her "improved" self.

> **What Others Say**
>
> Beauty—in projection and perceiving—is 99.9 percent attitude.
>
> —Grey Livingston

Esther was beautiful, in form and features (v. 7), and verse 15 shows that she still had her perspective intact. When it was her turn to appear before the king, she asked for nothing but what the king's eunuch suggested. She accepted the beauty routines, but she didn't become imbalanced. She retained her relationship with God; letting Him be the center of her life, not an obsession with transformation.

What makes a woman feel beautiful is the gaze of the observer. Women have a God-created need to be treasured and appreciated. As with every other part of life, the entrance of sin has warped this desire as well as a man's ability to meet it. The problem with the transformation culture is that it focuses on the wrong observer—man, not God.

Through the centuries, beauty has not been merely appreciated but manipulated to meet certain standards. Though there are some generally accepted points of beauty—symmetry of features, health, and well-proportioned body—the way beauty is evaluated changes with the centuries and with ethnic cultures. Given his desire to abuse what God creates, these beauty rules were probably engineered by Satan. Down through time, he has led the charge in mutilating, torturing, and maiming women in the name of beauty.

By getting women all bound up in trying to meet the fantastical standards of a fickle culture, Satan has succeeded in making them avoid the one observer they were created to please. In addition, he has driven men to such false expectations about women's beauty that they find it impossible to affirm the real women in their lives. The extreme, digitalized beauty seen in advertising and fashion photography distort the image of the loving observer. Men today are conditioned to rate women's beauty, rather than simply appreciating it. It is very difficult for a woman to feel authentic affirmation in such an environment.

Pornography is the ultimate false message about beauty, and our culture is being deluged with it. The Internet has realized Satan's dream of victimizing women by both false expectations of beauty and deprivation of fulfilling relationships. Men who ingest porn's message are poorly equipped to relate to a woman with normal flaws and a need for affirmation.

Pornography says all women are voluptuous, lustful, and always eager. Pornography is visual lies; it abuses women and devours men. Pornography was masterminded by Satan who has always offered a source of pleasure that circumvents God's plan.

Women have always been the pawn of beauty, but pornography trumps all of Satan's previous efforts. It is more insidious than the foot bindings of the Chinese, the lip plates worn by Suri women, and the broken ribs caused by corsets. Through porn, he destroys both women's

What Others Say

When I did my first adult film something very "dark" came over me. I could almost hear the devil say, "See Shelley, I will make you famous and THEN everyone will love you."

—Shelley Luben

bodies and spirits; he infects the relationships of both women and men. Pornography poisons God's plan for beauty. It turns the loving gaze of the observer into a predatory leer.

Eating disorders, extreme surgery, pornography . . . these are some of the by-products of transformation thinking. Satan's call to transformation is actually an invitation to disillusionment and enslavement.

The Word Speaks

God calls us to truth thinking—*the truth zone.*

TRUTH: My worth is not rooted in my appearance but in my relationship to God.

Examine 1 John 3:1. What word does John use to describe God's outpouring of love on us? God's love for us was not based on our performance or appearance. His desire for relationship springs from His deep love for us as His daughters, made in His image and redeemed by His Son. Why would it be offensive to God for me to base my self-worth on my appearance?

Recognizing my true worth means that I will accept myself as valuable just as I am, right now, without any changes. Discuss why that is difficult to do.

TRUTH: This body belongs to God. I should care for it appropriately.

Read Romans 12:1. The biblical image of a sacrifice is a helpless animal bound to an altar, giving its life to appease God's justice. Since Jesus was our substitute sacrifice for the atonement of sin, the spiritual sacrifice of our bodies is a way we offer Him our devotion. What does the descriptive word *living* tell us about the kind of sacrifice we are to be?

Read the quote from Adam Clarke's commentary. If a biblical sacrifice represented the choicest of a person's possessions, what does that tell us about the value God places even on our fallen physical bodies?

Bible Background

That ye present your bodies. A metaphor taken from bringing sacrifices to the altar of God. The person offering picked out the choicest of his flock, brought it to the altar, and presented it there as an atonement for his sin. They are exhorted to give themselves up in the spirit of sacrifice; to be as wholly the Lord's property as the whole burnt-offering was, no part being devoted to any other use.

—Adam Clarke

Since God's justice was forever appeased by His Son's death on the cross, what does the last part of the verse reveal as the purpose of our bodily sacrifice? We are to see our surrendered bodies as a means of *spiritual worship*. List some ways a woman can use her beauty to worship God.

The Bible talks quite a bit about *stewardship*. This is an old English word that means being a caretaker of someone else's valuable belongings, an assignment of a trust. First Corinthians 4:1–2 says, "So then, men ought to regard us as servants of Christ and as those entrusted with the secret things of God. Now it is required that those who have been given a trust must prove faithful."

How does stewardship of the body and its beauty differ from bondage to the culture's beauty messages? How have women of faith confused the two?

Where We Come In

As women of faith, think of some ways we struggle with our culture's philosophy of transformation.

The Bible does not specifically address the issue of cosmetic surgery. Why would motive play a role in this decision for a Christian woman? Is there a philosophical difference between having rhinoplasty (nose reshaping) and breast augmentation? Why or why not? Do you think there is a difference between having a surgical cosmetic procedure and tweezing the brows or shaping the nails? How would the biblical principle of monetary stewardship affect the decision to pursue cosmetic surgery?

How It Works Today

As a missionary in a third-world country, Julie was amazed to realize that women there struggled with the culture of beauty. When one takes into account the truth that women have an innate identity with beauty, it is not so surprising to find that every civilization has had beauty ideals. And with the infiltration of western lifestyle and fashion, women were further exposed to the glamour of transformation.

Julie's focus as a missionary was not only to bring the truth of God's love and forgiveness, but to instruct the women who, though different in some ways, still fought the same battles of worth and beauty. She started hosting small gatherings of women in her home where they had Bible studies and talked about women's issues. The meetings grew in attendance and blessed precious women who were enriched by Julie's heart for them. When she and her family returned to ministry in the States, Julie left behind a legacy of love and a strong sisterhood of women who continue to nurture each other in the truth.

Read Romans 12:2. Paul says to be "transformed by the renewing of your mind." Compare this with the transformation thinking of our culture. Satan's transformation message is a vicious cycle; God's transformation message is a liberating perspective. Discuss your thoughts.

Explain the contrast between the cultural motive of sex appeal and the scriptural motive of stewardship and worship as it pertains to beauty.

Responding through Prayer

Imagine a dedication service. There is to be a sacrifice—you. Instead of mounting the stone altar, you kneel before it. Your body is your willing gift to God, the loving Creator, Redeemer, and Observer. What would you say to Him at the moment? Say it to Him now.

My Next Step

This week, I will choose the correct zone—truth instead of transformation. I will honor the principles of consecration and stewardship by:

-
-

Keep It in Mind

We need to look at ourselves through God's perspective—it reveals the truth about our bodies and our worth. He is the One who helps us reject the illusion of transformation and the truth about our worth. He gives a crown of beauty instead of ashes, the oil of gladness instead of mourning, and a garment of praise instead of a spirit of despair" (Isa. 61:3).

5

The Warrior and the Princess

Proverbs 5:15–19

The man who finds a wife finds a treasure,
and he receives favor from the LORD.

—Proverbs 18:22 (NLT)

Discovery

Marriage was designed to celebrate and protect beauty.

For Openers

God designed marriage as the earthly representation of His relationship with His people, His bride, the Church. Satan is the antithesis of relationship; he preferred his own exaltation over a relationship with God. He is the embodiment of pride, and pride must ultimately dwell alone; it has no use for anyone but self. Because of this, Satan has mounted a vicious attack on marriage; God's symbol of His prized relationship with His people.

Through the sin of the first couple, Satan has achieved a twisting of natural desires. Men now struggle with selfish lust that is often directed at more than one woman. Many are wimpy about playing the warrior and doing the serious work of winning their wives' heart. Women now must contend with temptations of vanity and temptations to use their beauty to gain power over men. They tend to be too demanding—not trusting their husbands or respecting the hero God has given them.

From the beginning, God designed marriage as an exclusive covenant between two people. Genesis 2:24 says marriage is one man and one woman in a "one flesh" relationship. Furthermore, the bond of marriage represents God's own covenant with His people and, throughout Scripture, there are numerous references to God desiring the complete love of His people. Like any human spouse, He desires the full devotion of our love. This is why cheating on your mate offends God so much and why it is listed in the Ten Commandments. When a person commits adultery, she is tarnishing the symbolism of God's covenant with His people and embodying divided love. Jesus said the greatest commandment was to "Love the Lord your God will all your heart and with all your soul and with all your mind" (Matt. 22:37). It is impossible to do this with a divided love. The Old Testament used the imagery of adultery to symbolize the idolatry of the Israelites. They were literally cheating on God and giving their love to another. A marriage where the husband and wife are mutually devoted to each other results in a fulfilling relationship and a shining representation of God's covenant with us.

Getting to Know Her

When Solomon was young, he took a young Shulamite woman for his bride. Song of Solomon records their delightful romance. The young bride is nameless in Scripture, but she represents every woman—the dreams, the beauty, the love.

It seems she was from the countryside of ancient Israel. Verse 6 of the first chapter reveals that her skin had been darkened by the sun, which would not have happened to a woman of privilege. And it also refers to her working in the vineyards.

The Bible gives us a very intimate look into their love, and we can understand a little bit about how marriage celebrates beauty by examining this story.

> **What Others Say**
>
> The intensity of a man's ability to "notice" women was given to him so his wife would be attractive to him all the days of his life. His sexual eyes were intended to allow his wife to go through the natural changes that age and motherhood bring without her becoming unappealing to him.
>
> —Bill and Pam Farrel

The Word Speaks

Read Song of Solomon 4:1–7. These verses are the thoughts of a groom on his wedding day. In his love-filled eyes, his bride is totally beautiful. Her flaws seem inconsequential because of his desire for her (v. 7). To him, she is wondrously beautiful. Men were designed with vision that is programmed to notice female beauty. This was part of God's good creative work.

But sin has warped the human psyche. When Adam and Eve made the choice to sin, they had no way of realizing how their selfishness would corrupt the world they were leaving to future generations.

Every human desire and relationship was tainted by self-centeredness. Women are driven to gain admiration through provocative dress and behavior. Men are challenged by their compelling awareness of female beauty and the temptation to selfish gratification. And it isn't just a tendency to have "wandering eyes" that many associate with adolescent male behavior. This cognizance of beauty is actually chemical radar fashioned by a loving Father who wanted His daughters to be the object of wonder and delight. He intended a man to be intoxicated and emotionally exhilarated with the allure of his wife.

> Social science reveals a man's sexual response is initiated by his autonomic nervous system (ANS), which isn't controlled by the will, but by the environment. If a man sees a woman walk by wearing revealing clothing, his ANS can be activated. The brain then sends chemicals rushing through his body. He may notice the change in his pulse and his body temperature. While many men override these responses in a godly manner, they can't control their initial intoxicating reaction to an immodestly dressed woman. God intends for a man to enjoy this intoxicating power, but through only one woman—his wife.[1]

This natural reaction is constantly being exploited by the culture, and the result for marriages can be destructive. The wife's beauty will grow stale in her husband's eyes; others will look more attractive to him. The husband's lack of affirmation creates in his wife a need to reinvent herself; she falls prey to Satan's false messages.

Carefully read **Proverbs 5:15-19**.

The writer of Proverbs uses some very descriptive language in these verses to describe the intimate relationship of marriage. Clearly, he is saying that sexual love is to be cherished, private, and delightful. God intended that the beauty of the wife would draw the husband to her, fill his eyes, and cause him to admire and affirm her. Because they have made a commitment, they are to enjoy the one-flesh relationship that symbolizes the union of Christ and the Church—holy, eternal, and joyful.

Did You Know?

The phrasing of loving doe and graceful deer in verse 19 were metaphors of beauty and tenderness in ancient times.

Verse 16 refers to springs and streams of waters. Commentaries indicate this symbolizes the children which spring from the union of a man and woman.

Verse 15 refers to running water and verse 18 to a fountain. This imagery is not of a stagnant pool, but an ever-fresh source, a sparkling stream. A wife should be aware that letting their intimate life grow stale will create restlessness in her husband and make him more susceptible to temptation. While he must covenant with his eyes to stay focused on his wife (Job 31:1), the wife should recognize that God built into her man the spirit of an adventurer. He is designed to desire bigger challenges, fiercer battles, and greater triumphs. His warrior heart loves a conquest, in sex as well as in his career and recreation. "Your husband, like all men, lives for adventure, so if you are fulfilling that need in his life, he will be happier, easier to live with, more generous, and more motivated to please you."[2]

Bible Background

Let him that is married take delight in his wife, and let him be very fond of her, not only because she is the wife that he himself has chosen and he ought to be pleased with his own choice, but because she is the wife that God in His providence appointed for him and he ought much more to be pleased with the divine appointment, pleased with her because she is his own.

—Matthew Henry

Verses 18 and 19 encourage a husband to enjoy his wife and be intoxicated with her beauty and love. God is not a hater of beauty. How could He be? He invented and created it. He really wants women's beauty to be celebrated, admired, and affirmed. He has given husbands the ultimate privilege of doing this. That's why Proverbs 18:22 says a wife is visible proof of God's blessing. A bride is God's gift, His precious reward. That's how much God values His daughters.

Where We Come In

Life gets in the way of relationships. In the context of laundry and trips to the dentist and mortgage payments, celebrating beauty often gets neglected. A relationship between a husband and wife can be loving and secure but lack the element of delight.

Men have a difficult task, but God created them to be up to it. They are designed to be the head, the leader, the one who goes first. Look at 1 John 4:19. Using the biblical imagery of Christ and the Church, it seems to say that God has given husbands a big responsibility.

Men are called to be the lover, the wooer, the warrior. It isn't an easy thing in our culture to be the warrior of one woman's heart. Everything around a man today tempts him to indulge his proclivity to visual lust. It takes a stout-hearted adventurer to focus on the beauty of the one given to him by God. True, it is a challenge, but the male heart was crafted for this. He was created as the human image of righteous strength.

A practical way men can put this into practice is by verbal affirmation. It's one of the most challenging things for a man, but it is something that will prove he has a warrior heart and a spirit that will take up the challenge and do what is difficult to win the princess' heart.

Husband and wife team, Bill and Pam Farrel, say that a husband may grow weary of his wife's continuing need to hear that she is beautiful and valuable. He's said it before; why doesn't she believe him? He may even wish "she could process life more like a man while she continues to look like a woman."[3] But her feminine beauty cannot be separated from her feminine perspective. Maybe this is what Peter is referring to when he says, "In the same way, you husbands must give honor to your wives. Treat your wife with understanding as you live together" (1 Pet. 3:7 NLT). Honoring her need for affirmation is the loving kind of sacrificial leadership in which a husband is called to demonstrate his strength—the emotional kind.

A husband who loves his wife with his eyes and his words is something every woman desires, but wives often forget we have a related responsibility. Many men struggle with their challenge to love and to affirm. Many did not see it modeled before them in their own fathers, and certainly the culture has not done a good job in encouraging men to affirm their wives. Men often enter marriage without much mentoring in the skill of affirmation, in either words or affection. We cannot change our husbands, but we can make it easy for them to take up their challenge.

Read Genesis 3:1–7. When Eve sinned in Eden, she chose her own way above her dual authority—God and her husband. God had told Adam not to eat of the fruit from the tree in the center of the garden, and Adam had passed this on to his wife. We know this because of what she told the serpent. When she ate the fruit, she decided to put her will above God's. She also chose to bypass her husband's leadership by eating first and then talking to him. What do you think might have happened had she discussed it with Adam first?

In the same way, women now are tempted to choose their own comfort above their husband's pleasure. Life weighs us down with various home and work responsibilities. It is just so easy to look after ourselves and forget the priority of our husbands.

How It Works Today

Jean is an average woman who feels the pull of the culture on her relationship with her husband. Having been married for over twenty years, she has seen the effects of aging and childbearing on her body. Sometimes she contemplates cosmetic surgery, imagining a new and improved appearance. At other times, she feels contempt for the culture and its disparaging of women who don't fit the mold.

Walking through the mall, Jean wonders whether her scorn for the advertising posters in the windows is rooted in her indignation for the culture's disregard for modesty, or in her fragile self-worth that battles with measuring up or maybe in a sense of envy that others have an appeal she doesn't.

Involved in ministry as well as a wife and a mother, Jean has a full schedule that makes it challenging to enjoy romantic moments with her husband who is equally absorbed in Christian service. Sometimes the task of putting her husband first by making her appearance a priority seems overwhelming and less urgent in light of her obligations. Realizing that her beauty is the way God planned to bring her husband into deeper relationship has given Jean fresh motivation to invest in her marriage by finding authentic ways to enhance her attractiveness.

It may seem a trivial matter, but a wife's appearance is very important to her husband. Her beauty is God's gift to him. When she takes care to enhance her attractiveness, she is visibly showing love for her man. Once again, a woman is called to put self aside and show respect for her husband by pleasing him. We are called to do the difficult thing—to show love with disregard for our own comfort.

Extramarital affairs are powerful because they usually address the central needs of the man and woman involved. Married people don't usually get involved elsewhere because of physical desire alone. It is deeper than that. It is wrapped up in the strength and beauty bond. The illicit relationship feels valuable to a man because she makes him feel heroic (he needs admiration and respect). The woman is drawn to a forbidden lover because he makes her feel beautiful (she needs tenderness and affection).

Read Revelation 21:2. Again, God uses the imagery of a bride, and the wording implies the carefulness and lavishness of her preparation for her husband's eyes. In this verse, God is comparing the holy city, the place where God dwells, with a beautifully adorned bride, waiting to delight the heart of her groom. God placed in His daughters the knowledge of how to delight the man He has chosen for her. And Satan has seen to it that a woman battles the challenges of aging, fatigue, and time constraints. Take some time to discuss the satanic "conspiracy" against marriage and some practical ways to overcome it.

Read these vignettes.

- Dawn moved closer, looking up at the man standing next to her. He was so close to giving in. With a sweep of long lashes, she smiled at him. "Please. It's so good. You'll love it." She saw him hesitate and watched his surrender. He nodded and reached out his hand.

- Starr took a last look in the mirror. She did look pretty hot, but her husband was a hard man to please. He might even be angry when she interrupted him. Yet she had to let him know about the crisis and the only way to get his attention off his work and onto her was to wow him. She had to make him want to look at her so badly that he was willing to talk to her.

- Rue couldn't resist a twirl. The dress was gorgeous. Her heart was pounding at what she was going to do. The guy was mature, wealthy, and the town's most eligible bachelor. And he liked her. She knew he did. But she had waited long enough for a proposal. He needed motivation. She winked at her reflection. He was working late tonight; she would surprise him.

Would you be surprised if I tell you these scenes aren't from a steamy novel, but from the Bible? Would you feel differently about these women if I tell you their names are Eve, Esther, and Ruth?

Each of these women portrayed the power of feminine beauty. In their stories, beauty is depicted as compelling, captivating, and motivating. Eve's incomparable beauty blinded Adam's senses and he deliberately sinned. Esther's beauty caused the king to hold out the scepter to her and consequently grant protection to the nation of Israel. Ruth's beauty prompted a righteous man to offer her protection, marriage, and a place in the lineage of Christ.

Responding through Prayer

Spend a moment thanking God for the man He has given you. Ask God to help you put aside your own comfort to bless him with your beauty and to help you be creative in finding ways to delight his warrior heart.

If you are single, thank God for the strength of the men He has put in your life—father, grandfather, pastor, friends. Ask Him to affirm you through their counsel and friendship.

My Next Step

Read the biblical vignettes again. This week, how will you use your beauty to bless the man God has given you? Write down a couple ways:

-
-

Keep It in Mind

God expressed His strength in the creation of man; He displayed His beauty in the design of woman. Together, the warrior and the princess tell the tale of eternal love, representing God and His people, Christ and His Church. And God said it is good.

6

Kindred Spirits

Ezekiel 16:44; Ruth 3:1–3

May our sons flourish in their youth like well-nurtured plants. May our daughters be like graceful pillars, carved to beautify a palace.

—Psalm 144:12 (NLT)

Discovery

Daughters are a living legacy of the mother's perspective of beauty.

For Openers

Are You My Mother? Oh, the whimsical delight of Dr. Seuss! But tucked in this cutesy children's narrative is a scientific fact. When a gosling or duckling is hatched, it will identify with the first moving object it encounters. It's called *imprinting*. Researchers have determined that hatchlings will imprint with humans, another species of animal, or even an inanimate object like a white ball. They will follow the object and begin to mimic its behavior. And there isn't much time to get it right.

There is a limited window of time when effective imprinting can take place.

Just like babies in the animal world, daughters are affected by imprinting. From the woman who cares for her and models femininity, she learns what it means to be a woman. Obviously, this can be positive or negative. There used to be a little Sunday school song which had a line that said, "You can tell every girl by the kind of mom she's got."

There's truth to that statement. Although moms and daughters differ from each other in temperament and personal preference, the essence of femininity is passed from older women to younger women. Those who are imprinted negatively will struggle to find their role and identity as a woman.

Experiencing her daughter's journey of beauty is the privilege of a mother. Sometimes we are reminded of our own struggles—with self-esteem, blemishes, and body image. At other times, we are tempted to be envious of the freshness of youth and the admiration they receive. Putting our irritations aside and being an ally for our daughters will have a profound effect on them as they mature into women.

Getting to Know Her

What was it like to be a woman—a daughter—in ancient Israel?

Contrary to some perceptions, chauvinism is not a biblical theme. In fact, there are many indications otherwise, such as the deep love Abraham had for Sarah, and Isaac for Rebecca; the deference Elkanah showed to Hannah, and the sweet language of Song of Solomon in reference to the young wife.

Yet, because of selfishness and Satan's influence, there were some unfortunate effects on women in that time—they were rarely educated, could not converse with men publicly, and were often discriminated against by divorce for the most ludicrous reasons, such as burning the evening stew. (Jesus alluded to divorce in the Sermon on the Mount in Matt. 5:31.)

Of course, this was not God's will, but rather the complications caused by the entrance of sin into human relationships. Isn't it amazing to look back at history and see how Satan has encouraged the abuse and neglect of women and at the same time instigated the disintegration of the strength and leadership of men?

In reference to children, sons were preferred over daughters. Being a woman meant being subject to limitations—social and religious. But there was another reason.

The Jewish people knew the prophecy that a Savior would come. They knew He would be male—Messiah, the Holy One. God made a covenant with Abraham that he would father a great nation and that Messiah would be born through his descendants. Males carried in their physical bodies the seal of the Covenant—circumcision. When a baby boy was presented to the Lord and circumcised on the eighth day after his birth, his parents were making a statement to God—he was one of the chosen, one who would be marked by the Covenant for life. Every mother wanted to birth sons. They were the Covenant bearers.

Jesus showed true love and respect for the women He encountered during His earthly ministry. He broke protocol by speaking to the woman at the well (John 4:7). As He stumbled toward Golgotha, He turned to speak gently to the women who followed

Him; His thoughts were not on His suffering, but on what was to befall them in a few years (see Luke 23:28).

He modeled sacrifice and tenderness—what men are called to show in Ephesians 5:25–29. He spoke to women in gentle tones and with loving terms, often calling them "daughter."

Read the material about the woman who touched the hem of Jesus' garment. Why does this make you feel affirmed as a woman? Does this counteract any previous ideas you've had about the Bible and women?

What Others Say

No woman is mentioned as having spoken against Jesus in his life, or as having had a share in his death. Of woman born, by a woman was he anointed for his burial; a woman—Pilate's wife—pleaded for him, and here women wept over him. Women ministered to him in life, laid him in the grave, and were the first to meet him at his rising.

—*Spurgeon Devotional Commentary*

The Word Speaks

In the narrative where God compares His beloved Israel to a woman, there is a verse that addresses the mother-daughter relationship.

Read **Ezekiel 16:44**. "Like mother, like daughter." In allegorical terms, the Scripture is saying that the daughter Jerusalem was acting in identical ways to her "mother," the pagan nations who inhabited the land before the Jews. This proverb says that a daughter reflects her mother.

Just like the imprinting of ducklings, a mother is our earliest mirror of what womanhood is all about. In what ways do you see your mother in your appearance and manner? In what ways are you different from her?

Read Psalm 144:12. In this psalm, King David praises God for His protection and victory. He meditates on the brevity of life and the power of the Lord, then prays for deliverance for his nation and adds a wish for the sons and daughters of Israel.

David petitions God that the sons of the covenant may flourish "like well-nurtured plants." Like a forest preventing invasion, the young men of the nation should mature into stalwart leaders, standing between their families and the enemy.

And what about our daughters? They are to be like graceful "pillars carved to adorn [and beautify] a palace." We don't usually think of daughters as pillars; that seems an incongruous comparison.

Bible Background

The woman in Mark 5:25–34 who touched the hem of Jesus' garment had suffered a menstrual disorder for twelve years. According to Levitical law, she was ceremonially unclean (see Lev. 15:25–27). She was not to touch any sacred person or thing. She was likely anemic from years of blood loss. It took a great deal of effort for her to get close to the Master.

When she came up behind Jesus and touched the tassels of His garment, she was doing something unthinkable for a woman in that culture. For a woman, especially an unclean woman, to touch a man, a rabbi, was just not done. She had every right to fear when Jesus turned around and asked who had touched Him. The holy men of that day would have been incensed; Jesus was not. He called her "daughter" and assured her that her faith was valuable in His sight.

Incidentally, she was also making a profession of faith. She believed Jesus was Messiah. Ray Vander Laan says the Old Testament (in Malachi 4:2, for example) "prophesied that the Messiah would come with healing in his 'wings.' But the Hebrew word for 'wings' could also be used to identify the tassels that Jewish men wore on the corners of their robe. Based on this prophecy, the Jews expected the Messiah to have healing in his tassels."[1]

Yet, the psalmist seems to be expressing a twofold desire—that the young women of the nation would be the support that holds the family together and that they would adorn or grace the hearts and vision of those around.

Some commentators imply that David might have been referring to the Temple which had massive, elaborate foundation stones, and others think there is an interesting parallel in the architecture of other cultures.

It was common for ancient buildings to be supported with pillars. Look up Judges 16:26–30. Under God's anointing, Samson was able to collapse the mighty building where the Philistines were gathered by tumbling the two central pillars.

Samson had been tricked by two Philistine women—his wife who badgered him to learn the answer to a riddle for the profit of her countrymen, and Delilah

What Others Say

By daughters families are united and connected to their mutual strength, as the parts of a building are by the cornerstones; and when they are graceful and beautiful both in body and mind, they are then polished after the similitude of a nice and curious structure. When we see our daughters well established, and stayed with wisdom and discretion, as cornerstones are fastened in the building; when we see them by faith united to Christ, as the chief cornerstone, adorned with the graces of God's Spirit, which are the polishing of that which is naturally rough, and "become women professing godliness"; when we see them purified and consecrated to God as living temples, we think ourselves happy in them.

—Matthew Henry

The cornerstone of buildings in that day was prominent and eminent. Placed at the angle of the structure, where two walls met, on the top of the walls, and being richly ornamented and polished, it attracted attention.

—Samuel Martin

who toyed with his affections and betrayed him to his enemies. These women had been supporting the pagans with their feminine charm. Maybe they were in the crowd that perished that day; maybe not. But their power over Samson was ended. What they supported was wrong. The pillars crumbled. Discuss the possible symbolism between Samson breaking the two supporting pillars and the two Philistine women.

Did You Know?

"The polished corners of the temple", rather "the sculptured angles, the ornament, of a palace." Great care and much ornament were bestowed by the ancients upon the angles of their splendid palaces. It is remarkable that the Greeks made use of pilasters, called Caryatides (carved after the figure of a woman dressed in long robes), to support the entablatures of their buildings.

—Daniel Cresswell

Where We Come In

We are to instruct and guide our daughters that they may assume their God-given role in our society, that they can be the support and grace our culture needs. That means an understanding of the power of beauty in a woman's life.

Read the quote about *Little Women*. What do you think a mother can do to celebrate her daughter's beauty without encouraging her to feel "merely decorative?"

It is normal for girls to want to be pretty. Mothers want their daughters to be pretty. That's why we put bows in wispy baby hair and buy flouncy Easter dresses. Mothers know that little girls need to understand that being attractive is part of being feminine. But, as daughters enter the teen years, moms sometimes find themselves searching for the brakes. The culture has provided a very slick slope for our girls. Where they once coasted along with a giggle and smile, they now find a tricky highway that zooms along with a culture that isn't aligned with God's Word.

What Others Say

In the movie *Little Women*, there is a scene where Marmie is combing her daughter's lovely hair and says what I believe to be one of the most profound statements a mother can make to a daughter. "I only care what you think of yourself. If you feel your value lies in being merely decorative, I fear that someday you might find yourself believing that's all you really are. Time erodes all such beauty. But what it cannot diminish is the wonderful workings of your mind—your humor, your kindness, and your moral courage. These are the things I cherish so in you."

—Becky Freeman

So, it falls to us as mothers to guide them, to help them know how to be pretty and pure, charming and chaste. Yes, it's delicate; motherhood isn't for the fainthearted. We must come alongside them as kindred spirits. We must encourage them, instruct them, and celebrate them.

Read **Ruth 3:1–3**. This is the lovely story of Boaz and Ruth. Ruth had adopted Naomi as her mother when she left behind her own country and made a covenant to stay with Naomi the rest of her life. As her mother, Naomi instructs her in her relationship with Boaz.

Naomi tells Ruth what she should do. The NLT says it this way, "take a bath and put on perfume and dress in your nicest clothes" (v. 3). She tells her to go to where Boaz is hosting the harvest celebration and wait for him to lie down on the threshing floor. It was common practice for the master to sleep at the threshing floor to guard the harvest.

Naomi is careful to instruct Ruth in the ancient custom whereby a young girl could ask a man to "cover her" or give her protection through marriage. Naomi was a wise woman. She knew that to fulfill God's plan, a woman needs to look and act womanly, feminine, and attractive. When God creates a baby girl in the womb, He gives her life a plan which only a woman can fill. God's plan for Ruth was for her to marry Boaz. Naomi wanted her to look and smell wonderful to encourage Boaz toward a proposal. She didn't encourage Ruth to do anything inappropriate; she encouraged her to be feminine—attractive.

Mothers should do the same with their daughters. We can teach them the difference between being *attractive* (positive) and being *attracting* (negative). Using our beauty to gain lustful admiration or to preen our own pride is wrong. It gratifies self. It is a waste of God-given beauty. But celebrating our womanhood by looking attractive and feminine brings Him glory. It makes Him look good.

Our daughters will face a culture more imbalanced than we did. We need to teach them how to be beautiful in the context of the biblical principle that says the outside should be a reflection of the greater beauty that's inside. We need to spend as much time beautifying the inside as the outside, probably more. It will last longer.

Daughters take their cues from mom. If there isn't a good mother-daughter relationship, resentment will inhibit imprinting. List some ways you think a mom can improve the health of her relationship with her daughter.

Responding through Prayer

Pray this prayer for your daughter: *Father, thank You for giving me a daughter. Give me the wisdom to instruct her in being an attractive and godly young woman. I ask You for discernment so that I can sense when she is struggling and come alongside her as a kindred spirit. I ask You to make her a beautiful pillar that is supportive and graceful. Bless our relationship and help us both to be women who reflect Your beauty. In Jesus' name, Amen.*

How It Works Today

Sarah wants her daughters to be graceful pillars. As a speaker and a counselor, she knows the challenges women face. As a musician and photographer, she has a deep appreciation for beauty. As a pastor's wife, she has observed the treacherous path women walk, balancing Scripture and the culture. As a mom, she tries to look beyond the tantrums and the messes and teach her little ones the importance of their place.

Sarah and her husband have named their little boys Caiden ("warrior") and Corin ("spear"). They want their sons to be stalwart leaders, warriors who protect their sisters and who stand firm for God.

For their little girls, Kayla Rose ("pure rose") and Karissa Joy ("gift of joy"), they desire a beauty of soul and a gentle confidence in their value as women. Rather than being "merely decorative," Sarah wants her daughters to represent the glorious beauty of the One in whose image they were created. So, while she twists their little girl hair into pretty curls and encourages them to play dress-up, she also cultivates their awareness of the Father who delights in His daughters' beauty, no matter their age.

My Next Step

Plan some fun ways to celebrate your daughter's beauty and femininity. Add your own ideas to the list below.

- Go to a coffee shop, drink a latte, and talk about the season's styles—pros and cons.
- Go shoe and purse shopping—we're talking a real "girl thing" here.
-
-

Keep It in Mind

Daughters are a beautiful opportunity to leave a legacy in living form. Moms can help their daughters be like pillars to strengthen and adorn the kingdom of God.

"I have no greater joy than to hear that my children are walking in the truth" (3 John 4).

7

Girlfriend Glam

Genesis 29:16–35; 30:1–22

When they measure themselves by themselves and compare themselves with themselves, they are not wise.

—2 Corinthians 10:12

Discovery

Women need to support and celebrate each other's beauty.

For Openers

She wears a gorgeous dress, sits on the rolled-down top of a shiny car, and does the princess-wave all the way down Main Street. She is the beauty queen. And thousands of girls compete for the honor of being "the fairest of them all."

Even before they can flash a pearly baby tooth, miniature contestants take the stage. From infants to matrons and at every stage in between, pageants offer the chance for women to compete against each other, to be judged the most beautiful.

While competition can be healthy in some aspects of life, pitting women against each other in the beauty area has an unseen effect—it tears at the fabric of the girlfriend sisterhood. And every woman needs sisters, whether bonded by family or friendship.

The strength of sisterhood is an established fact. Most women I know do not enjoy activities alone. I see very few women eating by themselves in restaurants or enjoying a latte on their own. We may enjoy a solitary afternoon of reading, sure, but when it comes to going somewhere for fun, take a girlfriend with you.

Yet, the sisterhood is sometimes strained when it comes to affirming each other's beauty. There is this automatic measuring that takes place when women get together. Like men assessing a buddy's career or athletic prowess, women automatically ingest the details of another woman's appearance and grace and start to feel the effects of the comparison.

Getting to Know Her

Read **Genesis 29:16-35**. This is the tale of two sisters—Leah and Rachel. Leah was the older; Rachel the younger.

The Bible matter-of-factly states the difference between the sisters. We are given only one clue as to the outward looks of Leah—her eyes. Some translations render this description in verse 17 as weak or delicate eyes; some commentators say it means she had large, soft eyes; still others say she had blue eyes which were thought to be a blemish in that ancient culture. Whichever it was, it didn't compare with the exquisite beauty of Rachel who was appealing in both face and form. Jacob's manly sensibilities were intoxicated with the lovely younger sister, and he asked for her hand in marriage.

What follows must have been one of the cruelest tests of endurance for a woman, let alone a sister. Imagine a gorgeous wedding, an attentive groom, a night of beautiful intimacy . . . but you know a sickening secret—you are an imposter. The words your new husband whispers in your ear are really for your sister. The candlelight hides the fact from his eyes, and you feel like a criminal as you enjoy love that is not truly yours, no matter how legal it may be.

Consider how Leah felt in the morning light when her new husband turned to her in shock and says "You're not Rachel!" Then he storms out of the honeymoon tent and gives your father a few choice words for deceiving him.

Ponder how Leah felt when Jacob agreed to finish the bridal festivities (v. 27) out of duty to her. Wonder at her pain when her younger sister joins the "family" just a few days later. Then, try to understand the anguish wrapped up in the phrase that says "and he loved Rachel more than Leah" (v. 30).

The story continues as God blesses Leah with children. Motherhood was seen as a divine affirmation in those days and Leah has four sons in succession while Rachel is infertile. The names Leah chooses for her sons are significant.

Did You Know?

In ancient Israel, a child was named immediately after birth and the name was usually chosen by the mother. The custom of waiting for naming until circumcision on the eighth day is not noted until the New Testament era. To the Israelites, a name defined the essence of the thing and also reveals its character and destiny. The name might be chosen because of the particular circumstance of the birth or a characteristic of the child itself or even an event occurring at the time.

—Roland de Vaux

Feel her longing as she calls the firstborn Reuben which sounds like the Hebrew expression for "the LORD has seen my misery." She thinks surely her husband will love her now.

She names the second son Simeon ("one who hears") and the third son Levi ("attached"), hoping now her husband will be attached or bonded to her. Then she names the fourth son Judah ("praise"), giving thanks to the Lord for her children.

Now read **Genesis 30:1-22**. This tale of two sisters becomes complicated, an almost-war in the home of Jacob over his affections and his offspring. The sisters give their maids to their husband as concubines, a common practice in this culture where a pregnant maid was considered an extension of her mistress. As the child was being birthed, the mistress would kneel at the end of the birthing bed and the child would be delivered onto her lap. This ritual proclaimed that the child officially was the offspring of the mistress. Though she did not carry the child in her womb, she received "credit" for having a child. Imagine being so desperate for the affirmation of children that you would be willing to let a servant take your place in your husband's arms. That was the culture in which these women lived.

Back and forth, the sisters toss handmaids at Jacob in a struggle to have more children. Though Rachel was beautiful, she felt inferior because she was not fertile. So when her maid birthed a son, she said, "God has vindicated me" (v. 6) and when the maid birthed a second son, Rachel proclaimed, "I have had a great struggle with my sister, and I have won" (v. 8).

Read the quote by Ellery Queen. What do you suppose the atmosphere was like in Jacob's tents?

It gets even more complicated. Verses 14–16 tell the length of a sister's jealousy. When Leah's small son, Reuben, is out playing in the field, he finds some plants the Bible calls *mandrakes*. Scholars are unsure if these were herbs or pretty flowers. Some think the plant may have been believed to bring fertility. Others think they may have been pleasant to look at or smell. Maybe Reuben knew these were "special" plants, or perhaps he was like any little boy bringing flowers home to his mommy.

Rachel saw the mandrakes and wanted them. Leah is incredulous. "What? You not only steal my husband, but now you want to take away my little boy's flowers?"

Rachel really wants these things, so she makes a bargain. "OK, if you give me the mandrakes, you can have Jacob tonight."

> **What Others Say**
>
> The two women exchanged the kind of glance women use when no knife is handy.
>
> —Ellery Queen

Leah is quick to agree. When Jacob comes in from working hard that day, she goes out to meet him and tells him she has "hired" him for the night with her son's mandrakes. Probably not the greatest method of inducing a husband's desire!

Leah has two more sons and a daughter before finally God allows Rachel to conceive and give birth to a child—Joseph.

The Word Speaks

Look up Proverbs 14:30. The Bible says envy "rots the bones." Why does envy do this? One translation says envy is "like cancer in the bones" (NLT). Another says emotions like envy will "corrode the bones" (MSG). All of these words point to an inner

Bible Background

Both among the Greeks and Orientals this plant was held in high repute, as being of a prolific virtue, and helping conception; and from it philtres were made, and this is favoured by the meaning of the original, loves, i.e., incentives to matrimonial connections: and it was probably on this account that Rachel desired them.

—Adam Clarke

destruction. How could envy of another woman's beauty be destructive to emotional and spiritual health?

Rather than infect our friendships and sabotage our spiritual journey with the cancer of jealousy, the Bible presents a better way. That's what 1 Corinthians is all about: the best way to live—having Christ-like love. When God-centered love is the basis of our friendships, we are empowered to live beyond jealousy and envy. Look at 1 Corinthians 13:4, and catch what it says about envy. Why would it be impossible to live up to this under one's own power?

When Jesus was questioned about the greatest commandment, He gave a perfect answer: Love the Lord your God with all your heart, soul, and mind—your total being. And He added the companion commandment: Love your neighbor just like you love yourself (see Matt. 22:37–39).

What does that look like in twenty-first century skin? It means we should care for our sisters in faith just as much as we care for ourselves. That doesn't leave room for jealousy or envy. Real love wishes the best for others—not because it diminishes our own value, but because it rejoices or celebrates with the blessings of others.

Read Romans 12:15. The apostle Paul admonished his readers to rejoice with others who are rejoicing. How can this verse be applied in a very real way to girlfriend relationships, especially to others' body shape, skin type, hair color, wardrobe, etc.?

It is important to note that any woman feels twangs of appropriate jealousy when another woman dresses or conducts herself inappropriately in the presence of her husband. Celebrating a sister's beauty does not mean approving indelicate behavior. This is an entirely different matter.

As sisters in Christ, we have one final reason not to let another's beauty cause us to be jealous. As the body of Christ (and our sisters in faith fit the description!), we need to remember that one member's honor is every member's honor. Examine how Paul explained this in 1 Corinthians 12:14–26, especially noting verse 26.

How It Works Today

A group of women in northeastern Ohio have a real-life sisterhood. Like the popular novels by Robin Jones Gunn, they call themselves the *Sisterchicks*. They get together on a regular basis, frequently eating at a favorite restaurant and sharing their stories of what has happened during the week, laughing and crying together. They have a commitment to support and pray for one another in any crisis. They cheer each other on in various ministry passions such as pro-life counseling, Cystic Fibrosis aid, and other types of charity fund-raising. Together, they celebrate birthdays, Christmas, graduations, and everyday life.

These women experience life from differing viewpoints and have diverse tastes in style and contrasting preferences and personalities. Yet, they have found a way to affirm one another and to celebrate the unique beauty and gifts of each. Rather than comparing themselves, they focus on the extraordinary value of their girlfriends. And being together makes them even more beautiful.

Where We Come In

The sisterhood needs to celebrate, not critique; affirm, not assess; be genuine, not glib. Being a sister means more than being connected by DNA—Leah and Rachel proved that. Being a sister is a commitment to love, support, and celebrate.

Beneath our smiles, all women have insecurities. Every woman has or will have blemishes, bulges, wrinkles, gray hairs, and various other things we try so hard to hide. We're all in this thing together. If we place the emphasis on our flaws, we only strengthen the culture's power over us. It's when we build each other up that we lock arms and make each other more beautiful by our words and attitudes.

Read Proverbs 25:11. Women are particularly affected by words. God made us verbal and it is good—words are an important part of relationship, what we were created for. Sometimes our husbands don't fully understand our sensitivity to words, but our women friends do. We need to use our words to affirm and celebrate each other as women, as sisters in Christ. Think about how you can speak affirming words to the women in your circle of friends.

What Others Say

When sisters stand shoulder to shoulder, who stands a chance against us?

—Pam Brown

Responding through Prayer

Join hands with the women in your study group and pray together. Ask the Father to strengthen your friendships and give you the wisdom to affirm each other as women created in the unique and beautiful image of God.

My Next Step

Here are some ways I will share a little glam with a girlfriend this week:

-
-

Keep It in Mind

Read the quote by Pam Brown. Sisters in faith who celebrate each other's unique beauty will make the world a lovelier place. You go, girlfriend!

"Two people are better off than one, for they can help each other succeed" (Eccl. 4:9 NLT).

8

Beauty and the Body (of Christ)

Titus 2:4–5; 1 Peter 3:5–6; Proverbs 11:22

For this is the way the holy women of the past who put their hope in God used to make themselves beautiful.

—1 Peter 3:5

Discovery

The church should provide a biblical context that appropriately frames women's beauty.

For Openers

You're standing in front of your closet, trying to decide what to wear. Should you choose the new outfit that makes you feel attractive and feminine? Or is it wrong to like how you look? Maybe it is holier to be less coiffed. Can a woman who feels attractive also be godly?

On the other hand, should a woman insult the image of God in her by not presenting a pleasing reflection of His beauty? What are the boundaries? What is the biblical framework?

Women who turn to the church for clarification on the issue of beauty are often still confused. There has been much said in church about women's appearance, but not much from a positive aspect.

So, for women of faith, there is a conundrum. How do we balance the internal desire to be beautiful with a life lived for God's glory? Wanting to be pretty seems to be at odds with the traits of godliness that teach us to deny ourselves and have the humble mind of Christ. Is the pursuit of beauty compatible with a holy life? Can our inner enjoyment of being beautiful coexist with our love for Christ?

Some have felt that a pursuit of beauty was not compatible with a holy life. Throughout history, men of God have been baffled by the beauty question.

Augustine struggled to parallel his walk with God and his interaction with women. As a young man, he was sexually intemperate, feeling a slave to his own passions, living a promiscuous life. When he devoted himself utterly to God, he could not find a way to bring the two together. He continued to link womanly beauty with temptation. He referred to sexual impulses in negative terms and sadly lamented his lack of control. He could not see that beauty in women could be good. So, he dedicated himself finally to celibacy, remaining personally frustrated and influencing those who studied his writings.[1]

Balance is a difficult virtue for humans to achieve. We are lamentably prone to extremes. Women understand well that it is possible to be obsessed with the desire to be attractive. This imbalance is displayed in our culture on a daily basis.

But in responding to any societal gluttony, there is always the danger that the church will overreact. Acute disorder in our culture sometimes propels believers to other harmful extremes.

Excess is contrary to the Spirit-life taught in the Bible. Passages like Ephesians 5:18 and Titus 2:12, remind us not to be controlled by anything but to be led by the Holy Spirit. This applies to a beauty philosophy. So the value of restraint has long been recognized by women who are serious about reflecting God through their beauty. Unfortunately, history records that some in the church dismissed the "beauty thing" altogether, adopting a philosophy that a desire to be attractive must be a manifestation of self-centeredness. Some even went so far as to value women more for their maternal qualities than for their unique feminine nature and many seemed to believe that beauty was something to be feared and avoided.

Christian women should seek balance in this issue. A realistic look at both the creative design and the teachings of Scripture suggests that godliness and beauty can be seamlessly blended in the Christian woman's life.

Getting to Know Her

The first-century woman lived in a culture obsessed with the beauty of the female form. Their culture was amazingly comparable to ours in many ways. Sculptures and paintings were devoted to portraying the human body. The Roman baths were a testament to the ancients' fastidious grooming. The elaborate hairstyles of Roman women were more than decorative; they were powerful statements about the wearer.

In addition, the Roman attitude toward sexuality was casual. Love and sex were separated in the Roman mind; emotional attachment might be part of the experience, but it wasn't necessary. Sexuality was viewed as a merely human urge which could be met at one of the many brothels in every community. Even Roman worship was rife with sexuality, as the pagan temples employed religious prostitutes who were available for the pleasure of the worshipers. There seemed to be no social stigma in taking advantage of these sources.

Did You Know?

A woman with an exquisite hairstyle was at once attractive and also virtuous. Empresses and princesses worked with their hairstylists to create new coiffures because they wanted to be perceived as fashionable, on the cutting edge, and prosperous, but, at the same time, these hairstyles proclaimed that their wearer possessed all the traits desirable in the ideal Roman woman. In addition, these hairstyles were not chosen haphazardly. Instead, each corkscrew curl, each flowing tress, and each blunt cut bang was carefully arranged to make reference to the political or social agenda of the current dynast and his family.

—Diana E. E. Kleiner and Susan Matheson

Using this backdrop gives us a new perspective on the women of the New Testament era and the writings of the apostles. There had come into being in Roman culture what is sometimes referred to as the "new wife" or "new woman."[2] This term represents those women living in the first-century A.D. who had embraced new social mores as exhibited in manner and dress. They were the visual aid for the Roman obsession with beauty and sexuality.

It is likely that because of the cultural obsession with outward appearance, the New Testament references to women in the early church do not highlight their beauty, but focus on their other admirable qualities. Every day in the marketplace, New Testament women were bombarded with messages about beauty. Through the letters of the apostles, God was trying to bring balance to these women, who like us, faced incredible pressure from the society to embrace beauty without boundaries.

The Word Speaks

The church needs to present a balanced message to God's daughters. It should neither smother their God-given beauty, nor should it encourage a narcissistic attitude.

Read **Titus 2:4-5**. The word translated "self-controlled" is defined "discreet" in the King James Version. Look up the word *discreet* in a dictionary. Which definition do you think applies to this verse?

Now read **Proverbs 11:22**. This verse combines the attribute of discretion with beauty. More than simply saying a beautiful woman should also be wise, these words connect the two. There cannot be true beauty without discretion; discretion is that delicate respect for something of high value that protects and keeps. A woman who claims beauty but has no discretion is mistaken; hers is merely pretty wrappings, not beauty. Just as a golden ring is not valued by a pig, a woman who has no discretion does not recognize the worth of her beauty. She will be muddied by the warped culture.

So, the older women are to mentor the younger women in this sense of discretion which obviously applies to their personal beauty as well as to their other character qualities.

The next trait which the apostle Paul admonishes women to embody is purity or chastity. As we have seen from the historical context, this concept was disparaged then, just as it is in our culture. Sexuality was exhibited, flaunted, and paraded through the public square. But our Father calls His daughters to model the lovely grace of purity which provides the proper frame for beauty.

Now look at **1 Peter 3:5**. God's Word says a woman will only discover her true beauty when her motive and her response to authority are right.

We've seen God's heart for His daughters: He gives them beauty and asks that they surrender it back to Him as a means of worship. That is how we can imitate the holy women of old in trusting God.

What about the authority aspect? Submission is a gift only a woman can give. Men can have a servant's heart, but they cannot be submissive in the way a woman can. They were not created to be; women were.

What Others Say

We've been cut to a certain size and shape to fulfill a certain function. It is this, not that. It is a woman's offering, not a man's, that we have to give.

—Elisabeth Elliot

Bible Background

That the woman was made of a rib out of the side of Adam; not made out of his head to rule over him, nor out of his feet to be trampled upon by him, but out of his side to be equal with him, under his arm to be protected, and near his heart to be beloved.

—Matthew Henry

God made a special place for women—a place of cherishing and protection—within the physical, emotional, and spiritual strength of a man. It is not to stifle or to abuse her, but to care for her. It is the design for a relationship conceived in the very heart of God who does all things well.

Read the words of Matthew Henry on the creation of woman. Describe your reaction to these words.

Where We Come In

When a girl is young, her hero and protector is her father. When she is married; this position is transferred to her husband. Women who rebel against their God-placed authority cannot discover and celebrate their true beauty. They may possess physical attractiveness, but it does not nourish or bless those around.

Sarah, Abraham's wife, knew the secret of real beauty. Look up Genesis 12:11. Abram is afraid that the Egyptians will kill him so the Pharaoh could have Sarai, his wife, because she was a beautiful woman. Now, look at Genesis 12:4. How old was Abram when he was called by God to leave Haran? Genesis 17:17 tells us that Sarai was ten years younger than Abram. What would that make her age when she was traveling with her husband through the land of the Egyptians?

A woman who is beautiful at that age (so gorgeous a king wanted her for his harem) is unusual even in our culture with all of our cosmetics, spas, and surgeries. Imagine how incredible it was for a nomadic woman who lived in a tent in the desert!

Read **1 Peter 3:6**. Do you think it is possible that Sarah's beauty was actually enhanced by her gracious acceptance of her God-given place? What challenges do we face in imitating her?

How would recognizing her God-given authority have a bearing on a woman's approach to beauty?

Think about how some men in the church insult their sisters in Christ when they publicly eulogize godly beauty and privately ingest pornography. In what ways has this hypocrisy affected the voice of the church on the subject of beauty? Read this statement: *Men in the church may be hesitant to address the beauty issue honestly because of their own struggles with lust and because it is easier to blame someone else than accept responsibility.* Do you agree? Name some ways the church can address this problem. How can a woman avoid becoming so suspicious of men in general that she doesn't trust the integrity of the ones with whom she worships?

The body of Christ has sometimes overreacted to the beauty issue. At other times, it has not provided appropriate instruction. How can the church today present a balanced perspective?

Responding through Prayer

Father, guide Your church to affirm and instruct the women within it. Please protect Your daughters from being shaped into the culture's idea of beauty. Work in me the grace of discretion and a submissive attitude to the authority You have placed in my life. I want my motive to be pure and my beauty to bring You praise. Let me bless the body of Christ with my gifts and presence. In Your Son's name, Amen.

My Next Step

The church needs its daughters to model authentic beauty framed by discretion and purity. In my local church, I will:

-
-

Keep It in Mind

As sisters in faith, we are the Church's representatives to a culture addicted to destructive beauty messages. We are privileged to model the Creator's awesome design.

> Many women have done wonderful things, but you've outclassed them all! Charm can mislead and beauty soon fades. The woman to be admired and praised is the woman who lives in the Fear-of-GOD. Give her everything she deserves! Festoon her life with praises! (Prov. 31:29–31 MSG)

How It Works Today

Michael and his wife Lori minister in a small church in a mid-western suburb. As a husband and a pastor, Michael is concerned with the imbalance sometimes projected in the church's teaching about women's beauty. As a man, he knows that men need their wives to be attractive. As a pastor, he has witnessed the excesses of the secular culture. He thinks the church should help women as they try to bridge the gap between the two extremes.

Michael admits that the church has sometimes failed God's daughters by not giving them balanced instruction and affirmation in the area of beauty. In his relationship with his wife and in training his daughters, Michael tries to model the appropriate perspective—celebrating their beauty and teaching Scriptural perimeters. He believes the church should provide a biblical context that properly frames feminine beauty as a shining reflection of the image of God.

Notes

Chapter 1

1. John and Stasi Eldredge, *Captivating* (Nashville: Thomas Nelson, 2005), 84.

Chapter 5

1. Dannah Gresh, "A Decent Proposal," *Today's Christian Woman* (May/June 2003, vol. 25, no. 3), 46. Also available at http://www.christianitytoday.com/tcw/2003/mayjun/3.46.html.
2. Bill and Pam Farrel, *Red Hot Monogamy* (Eugene, Ore.: Harvest House Publishers, 2006), 118.
3. Ibid., 197.

Chapter 6

1. That the World May Know Ministries, "The Tassels," http://www.followtherabbi.com/Brix?pageID=2089.

Chapter 8

1. Karen Lee-Thorp and Cynthia Hicks, *Why Beauty Matters* (Colorado Springs: NavPress, 1997), 201–204.
2. Bruce W. Winter, *Roman Wives, Roman Widows: The Appearance of New Women and the Pauline Communities* (Grand Rapids, Mich.: Wm. B. Eerdmans Publishing Co., 2003), 5.